To:

Mom

From:

Lexi

Date:

5/13/12

ISBN 978-1-61626-621-9

Written and compiled by Nanette Anderson in association with Snapdragon Group℠, Tulsa, OK.

Cover and interior design: Connie Gabbert, conniegabbertdesign.com

Published by Barbour Publishing, Inc., P.O. Box 719, Uhrichsville, Ohio 44683, www.barbourbooks.com

Our mission is to publish and distribute inspirational products offering exceptional value and biblical encouragement to the masses.

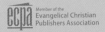

Member of the
Evangelical Christian
Publishers Association

Printed in China.

MOM

❋❋

Magnificent
One -of-a- kind
Multi-Talented

BARBOUR
PUBLISHING

Most of all the other beautiful things in life
come by twos and threes, by dozens and
hundreds. Plenty of roses, stars, sunsets,
rainbows, brothers and sisters,
aunts and cousins, comrades and friends—
but only one mother in the whole world.

KATE DOUGLAS WIGGIN

Contents

One lamp—

thy mother's love—

amid the stars

shall lift its pure flame

changeless, and before

the throne of God,

burn through eternity

holy—as it was lit

and lent thee here.

Nathaniel Parker Willis

Celebrating a Mother's Love

There is religion
in all deep love,
but the love of a mother
is the veil of a softer light,
between the heart and
the heavenly Father.

SAMUEL TAYLOR COLERIDGE

A Special Love

As a loving mother, you are more valuable
than all the world's combined wealth.
No one loves as freely and unconditionally
as you do. All other love is tinged with at
least a glimmer of self-interest, but not
yours. You see your child as part of yourself
and thus you love with reckless abandon—
completely, unconditionally.
Indeed, as a mother, you would be willing
to give your life without hesitation for the
sake of your child. The way you love your
children is God's gift. He has instilled it
in your genes. So embrace it, cherish it,
let it see you through the tough times and
bring you joy in the good times. You are a
mother! What a job! What a privilege!

We love because [God] first loved us.

1 JOHN 4:19 NRSV

Some mothers are kissing
mothers and some are scolding
mothers, but it is love just the
same, and most mothers kiss
and scold together.

PEARL S. BUCK

May God's hand
strengthen your heart and
cause your mother's love to
overflow each day, each hour,
each minute, as you embrace the
blessed job He has given you.

Heavenly Father,
Keep my love for my
children strong and vibrant.
Help me to make tough
choices regarding them—
choices that will help them
avoid misfortune and live
good lives filled with
rich blessings.
Amen.

Who is it that loves me
and will love me forever
with an affection which no
chance, no misery, no crime
of mine can do away?—
It is you, my mother.

Thomas Carlyle

A mother's love and prayers
and tears are seldom lost on
even the most wayward child.

A. E. DAVIS

[Love] always protects,
always trusts, always hopes,
always perseveres.
Love never fails.

1 CORINTHIANS 13:7–8 NIV

There is no friendship,
no love, like that of the
mother for the child.

HENRY WARD BEECHER

"Isn't there one child
you really love the best?"
a mother was asked.
And she replied, "Yes.
The one who is sick until
he gets well; the one who's
away, until he gets home."

Unknown

As you pour your love out
on your children, may your
mother's heart be filled again
with the love of God.

A mother's love for the child
of her body differs essentially
from all other affections,
and burns with so steady and
clear a flame that it appears
like the one unchangeable
thing in this earthly mutable
life so that when she is no
longer present, it is still
a light to our steps
and a consolation.

W. H. HUDSON

The name of mother!
The sweetest name that
gently falls on mortal ear!
The love of mother!
Mightiest love which
heaven permits
to flourish here.

UNKNOWN

Maternal love: a miraculous substance
which God multiplies as He divides it.

VICTOR HUGO

Thou art thy mother's glass,

and she in thee

calls back the lovely

April of her prime.

WILLIAM SHAKESPEARE

Heavenly Father,
Thank You for
entrusting me with children.
They have brightened
my days and given my life
purpose. May they always
know how much
I love them.
Amen.

A mother's love is so strong
and unyielding that it endures
any and all circumstances:
good times and bad,
prosperity and deprivation,
even honor and disgrace.

UNKNOWN

Mother love is the fuel that
enables a normal human
being to do the impossible.

MARION C. GARRETTY

A mother's love perceives

no impossibilities.

CORNELIA PADDOCK

There is in all this world

no fount of deep,

strong, deathless love,

save that within

a mother's heart.

FELICIA HEMANS

May your father and mother rejoice;
may she who gave you birth be joyful!

PROVERBS 23:25 NIV

A Memory

A picture memory bring to me:

I look across the years and see

Myself beside my mother's knee.

I feel her gentle hand restrain

My selfish moods, and know again

A child's blind sense of wrong and pain. . . .

But wiser now,

A man gray grown,

My childhood's needs are better known,

My mother's chastening love I own.

JOHN GREENLEAF WHITTIER

Mother is the name
for God in the lips and
hearts of children.

WILLIAM MAKEPEACE THACKERAY

A mother's love is an
early taste of heaven.

Heavenly Father,

Take the love I have given my children
and create in them hearts filled with love
for their own children.

Amen.

Love begins by taking
care of the closest ones—
the ones at home.

MOTHER TERESA

Lying there after her ordeal,
with the baby on her arm,
she knew the age-old surge
of mother love. All her old love
of life seemed to concentrate
on one thing—the little soft,
helpless bundle.

BESS STREETER ALDRICH

God knows a mother needs
fortitude and courage and
tolerance and flexibility and
patience and firmness and
nearly every other brave
aspect of the human soul.

PHYLLIS MCGINLEY

Celebrating a Mother's Courage

Sometimes the strength
of motherhood is greater
than natural laws.

BARBARA KINGSOLVER

It Takes Guts!

By nature, mothers are courageous.
They encounter and overcome the
innumerable challenges of a sick child,
a strong-willed child, the testy adolescent,
the slow-to-leave-the-nest adult. They send
their children out in cars, off to school,
into the workplace, on dates, and away to
college. Mothering is joy, yes! It is blessing
and fulfillment, yes! But it is not for the
weak-hearted! Ask God for the courage
it will take to complete the job.

*Wait for the LORD; be strong and
take heart and wait for the LORD.*

PSALM 27:14 NIV

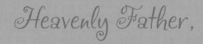

Heavenly Father,

Thank You for investing in me the
courageous heart of a mother.
Help me to always be strong and daring
for my children, ready to defend them
at a moment's notice, just as You
have always defended me.

Amen.

Living is risky,
and so is being a mother.
But it's better to draw up your
courage and plunge in than to
miss out on the avalanche of
blessing that comes from both.
As you know by now,
some risks are well worth taking.

Making the decision to
have a child is momentous.
It is to decide forever to have
your heart go walking around
outside your body.

ELIZABETH STONE

The sweetly sung lullaby; the cool hand on the fevered brow; the Mother's Day smiles and flowers are only a small part of the picture. True mothers have to be made of steel to withstand the difficulties that are sure to beset their children.

RACHEL BILLINGTON

*Act with courage,
and may the LORD be
with those who do well.*

2 CHRONICLES 19:11 NIV

A mother's sacrificial, unconditional love for her children creates in her a determined ferocity to protect and prosper them that transcends human understanding. And for the child, this unbridled bravery is an asset beyond human calculation!

No language can express the power and
beauty and heroism of a mother's love.

Edwin H. Chapin

You may have others who will be more demonstrative but never who will love you more unselfishly than your mother or who will be willing to do or bear more for your good.

CATHERINE BRAMWELL BOOTH

Moms are fearless!
They remain cheerful when the
lights go off, calmly explain
that the sounds outside the
window are just tree branches
blown by the wind, and check
under the beds for monsters
every night. Moms have courage
for the ordinary and
extraordinary issues of life.

My mother. . .taught
me about the power of
inspiration and courage,
and she did it with a
strength and a passion that
I wish could be bottled.

Carly Fiorina

Thank you, Mom,
for brushing away my fears
and showing me how to
face the world with a smile.

It's not easy being a mother.
If it were easy,
fathers would do it.

FROM THE TELEVISION SHOW
THE GOLDEN GIRLS

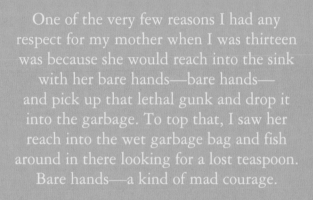

One of the very few reasons I had any
respect for my mother when I was thirteen
was because she would reach into the sink
with her bare hands—bare hands—
and pick up that lethal gunk and drop it
into the garbage. To top that, I saw her
reach into the wet garbage bag and fish
around in there looking for a lost teaspoon.
Bare hands—a kind of mad courage.

ROBERT FULGHUM

Heavenly Father,

Help me to face each new
day with the courage and
strength of my convictions
that I may set a virtuous
example for my children.

Amen.

Sometimes when our hearts grow weary,

or our task seems very long;

When our burdens look too heavy,

and we deem the right all wrong.

Then we gain a new, fresh courage,

as we rise to proudly say:

"Let us do our duty bravely,

This, you know, was Mother's way."

ABRAM JOSEPH RYAN

Do not ask God for a life free from grief; instead ask for courage that endures.

UNKNOWN

There never was a woman like
her. She was gentle as a dove
and brave as a lioness. . . .
The memory of my mother
and her teachings were,
after all, the only capital I had
to start life with, and on that
capital I have made my way.

ANDREW JACKSON

I was afraid of strangers until
I saw you smiling at them.
I was afraid to cross the street
until you took my hand and led
me across with confident strides.
I was afraid to love until I
saw you recover from love lost.
You taught me to be brave,
Mom. I'll always be grateful.

A mother laughs our laughs,
sheds our tears,
returns our love,
fears our fears.
She lives our joys,
cares our cares,
and all our hopes
and dreams she shares.

UNKNOWN

*A woman giving birth to a child has
pain because her time has come;
but when her baby is born she forgets
the anguish because of her joy that
a child is born into the world.*

JOHN 16:21 NIV

A mother is a blend of
strength and survivorship,
experience and insight,
fancy, and reflection.

UNKNOWN

Thank you for having
the courage to raise me.
Being responsible for
another person's life is
a scary proposition,
but you never wavered.

Mama was my
greatest teacher, a teacher
of compassion, love,
and fearlessness.
If love is sweet as a flower,
then my mother is that
sweet flower of love.

STEVIE WONDER

Let us not become weary
in doing good, for at the
proper time we will reap a
harvest if we do not give up.

GALATIANS 6:9 NIV

Heavenly Father,

Help me as I encourage my
children to boldly pursue
the gifts and talents You
have placed in their lives.
I want to see them become
all they were created to be.

Amen.

I have been told that my mother,
when she surmised from the face of the
physician that her life and that of her child
could not both be saved, begged him to
spare the child. So through these many
years of mine, I have seldom thanked
God for His mercies without
thanking Him for my mother.

JAMES M. LUDLOW

Mothers brave much heartache but they never give up, and their courage has at times made all the difference in their children's lives. It's as if they are saying, "If my mom believes in me, shouldn't I believe in myself?"

Rule #10

Never get between
a bear and her cub;
a bird and her nest;
or a mother and her child.
You'll regret it.
These creatures are prepared
to fight to the death.

NANCY GARTH

A little boy's mother once told him that it is God who makes people good. He looked up and replied, "Yes, I know it's God, but mothers help a lot."

Celebrating a Mother's Work

The phrase "working mother"
is redundant!

JANE SELLMAN

The Greatest Profession

We've all heard the phrase, "A mother's work is never done!" It's true. When her children are small, there are clothes to fold, science projects to oversee, lunches to make. Mom is there, getting it done. And when her children are grown, the list, though it changes, is barely diminished.
For a mother, there are no vacations and no sick days. From the day her children are born until she takes her last breath, they are her primary concern. But she glories in it. For she understands why she labors. The world is counting on her.

"There are many virtuous and capable women in the world, but you surpass them all!"

PROVERBS 31:29 NLT

*If evolution really works,
how come mothers only
have two hands?*

MILTON BERLE

The life of a working mother
who lives without the constant
presence and support of the
father of her children works
three times harder than any
man I have ever met.

GOLDA MEIR

By and large, mothers and
housewives are the only
workers who do not have
regular time off.
They are the
vacationless class.

ANNE MORROW LINDBERGH

I looked on childrearing not only as a work of love and duty, but as a profession that was fully as interesting and challenging as any honorable profession in the world and one that demanded the best that I could bring it.

ROSE KENNEDY

Heavenly Father,

Make my day productive,
for I know the work You
have given me is of great
importance. I look to You
to bless every moment
and every hour with Your
encouraging presence.

Amen.

The first job of
a mother is to work
herself out of a job.
If she succeeds she
will enjoy the rewards
for a lifetime.

UNKNOWN

Any mother could perform
the jobs of several air-traffic
controllers with ease.

LISA ALTHER

To be a mother is a woman's greatest
vocation in life. She is a partner with God.
No being has a position of such power
and influence. She holds in her hands the
destiny of nations, for to her comes the
responsibility and opportunity of
molding the nation's citizens.

SPENCER W. KIMBALL

Motherhood cannot finally be delegated. Breast-feeding may succumb to the bottle; cuddling, fondling, and pediatric visits may also be done by fathers. . . but when a child needs a mother to talk to, nobody else but a mother will do.

ERICA JONG

The most important occupation
on earth for a woman is to be
a real mother to her children.
It does not have much glory
to it; there is a lot of grit and
grime. But there is no greater
place of ministry, position,
or power than that of a mother.

PHIL WHISENHUNT

There was never a
great man who had not
a great mother.

OLIVE SCHREINER

When you are a mother,
you are never alone
in your thoughts.
You are connected to your
child and to all those who
touch your lives. A mother
always has to think twice,
once for herself and
once for her child.

SOPHIA LOREN

Mothers are the most unselfish,
the most responsible people in the world.

BERNARD M. BARUCH

Mom, you are the best—
best friend, best advisor,
best confidante, best mom.
Thank you for working hard
to help me become the very
best me I can be.

Heavenly Father,
Thank You for all the
responsibilities of motherhood
and all the blessings.
It's so good to know that
we're in this thing together.
Amen.

I depended on my mother for everything. I watched her become a strong person and that had an enormous influence on me.

ROSALYNN CARTER

As a mother, my job is
to take care of the possible
and trust God with
the impossible.

RUTH GRAHAM

We are labourers
together with God.

1 CORINTHIANS 3:9 KJV

A man's work is from sun to sun,
but a mother's work is never done.

UNKNOWN

The future destiny of the
child is always the work
of the mother.

NAPOLEON

Mother, you wrote no lofty
poems that critics consider art;
but with a nobler vision,
you lived them in your heart.

THOMAS FESSENDEN

Upon the mother devolves the duty of planting in the hearts of her children those seeds of love and virtue which shall develop useful and happy lives. There are no words to express the relation of mother to her children.

A. E. DAVIS

Every mother is like Moses;
she does not enter
the promised land.
She prepares a world
she will not see.

POPE PAUL VI

A mother has, perhaps, the hardest earthly
lot; and yet no mother worthy of the name
ever gave herself thoroughly for her child
who did not feel that, after all,
she reaped what she had sown.

HENRY WARD BEECHER

The mother who does her
part in rearing and
training aright the boys
and girls who are to be
the men and women of
the next generation. . .
is more important by far
than the successful
statesman or businessman
or artist or scientist.

THEODORE ROOSEVELT

The mother in her office
holds the key of the soul;
and she it is who stamps
the coin of character.

ELLA S. HOPSON

My mother was the source
from which I derived the
guiding principles of my life.

JOHN WESLEY

Celebrating a Mother's Wisdom

A mother understands
what a child does not say.

JEWISH PROVERB

All the Answers

From the very moment of birth, children
depend upon their mothers to have all the
answers. When they are toddlers, they venture
out and then come running back to the one who
knows what they don't. In adolescence,
children wish you didn't know as much as you do;
they pretend you don't. In adulthood, they come
to appreciate your wisdom and counsel.
It's not easy when others expect you to have all the
answers. It means looking to God for Wisdom.

*Wisdom is a tree of life
to those who embrace her;
happy are those who hold her tightly.*

PROVERBS 3:18 NLT

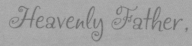

Heavenly Father,

Give me the wisdom to be the best mother
possible for my children. Help me know
when to hold on and when to let go.
Help me teach them the skill of making
good choices all along the way.

Amen.

A daughter is a
mother's gender partner,
her closest ally in the
family confederacy,
an extension of her self.
And mothers are their
daughters' role models,
their biological and emotional
road maps, the arbiters of
all their relationships.

VICTORIA SECUNDA

Never lend your car
to anyone to whom you
have given birth.

ERMA BOMBECK

When she speaks, her words
are wise, and she gives
instructions with kindness.

PROVERBS 31:26 NLT

My mom instilled a lot of
values about living in me—
what's right and what's
wrong. She made me feel
safe about the world.

DENNIS QUAID

A mother. . . .will cling to us, and endeavor by her kind precepts and counsels to dissipate the clouds of darkness and cause peace to return to our hearts.

WASHINGTON IRVING

105

A mother is the thread
that ends a broken heart.

UNKNOWN

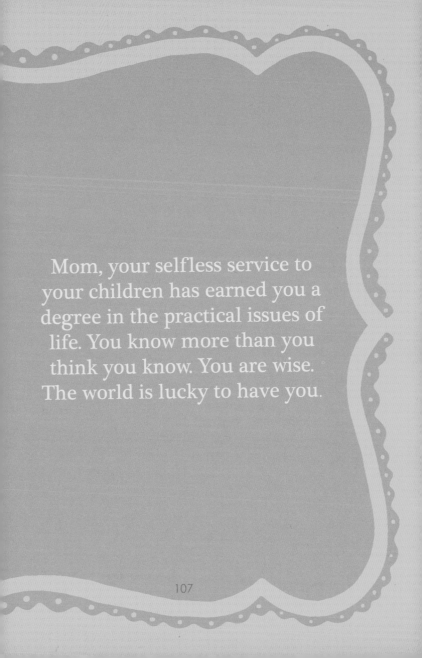

Mom, your selfless service to your children has earned you a degree in the practical issues of life. You know more than you think you know. You are wise. The world is lucky to have you.

The bearing and training of a child is women's wisdom.

LORD TENNYSON

*Most mothers are
instinctive philosophers.*

HARRIET BEECHER STOWE

Education commences at the mother's knee, and every word spoken within the hearing of little children tends toward the formation of character.

HOSEA BALLOU

Motherhood is the greatest
potential influence in human society.
Her caress first awakens in the child
a sense of security; her kiss the first
realization of affection; her sympathy
and tenderness, the first assurance
that there is love in the world.
Thus in infancy and childhood
she implants ever-directing and
restraining influences that
remain through life.

DAVID O. MCKAY

I shall never forget my mother, for it was she who planted and nurtured the first seeds of good within me. She opened my heart to the lasting impressions of nature; she awakened my understanding and extended my horizon, and her percepts exerted an everlasting influence upon the course of my life.

IMMANUEL KANT

A mother is one to
whom you hurry when
you are troubled.

EMILY DICKINSON

The best advice from my
mother was a reminder to
tell my children every day:
"Remember you are loved."

EVELYN MCCORMICK

Heavenly Father,
I look to You for the
wisdom I need to raise
my children properly.
Help me to understand
them and their gifts
and convey to them the
principles they will need
to be successful.
Amen.

I want to thank you, Mom,
for all the good advice and
wise words you've given
me through the years.
I thank God for a
mother like you.

You created my inmost being;
you knit me together in my
mother's womb. I praise you
because I am fearfully and
wonderfully made;
your works are wonderful,
I know that full well.

PSALM 139:13–14 NIV

Blessed are the
mothers of the earth.
They combine the practical
and the spiritual into
the workable ways
of human life.

WILLIAM L. STINGER

The mother, more than any other, affects the moral and spiritual part of the children's character. She is their constant companion and teacher in formative years. The child is ever imitating and assimilating the mother's nature.

E. W. CASWELL

My mother is my teacher,
adviser, and greatest inspiration.

WHITNEY HOUSTON

If any of you lacks wisdom,
you should ask God,
who gives generously to all
without finding fault,
and it will be given to you.

JAMES 1:5 NIV

Heavenly Father,
Thank You for
giving me the wisdom
I need when I need it.
I look to You to help me
be the best mom I can be.
Amen.

Motherhood is a
partnership with God.

UNKNOWN

Mom, you may have
wondered if the wisdom
you shared with me was
wasted. It wasn't.
Though it may have
seemed like it had little
effect at the time,
your words stayed with me.
Your words helped me
find the answers I needed.

Train children in the
right way, and when old,
they will not stray.

PROVERBS 22:6 NRSV

My mother had a great
deal of trouble with me,
but I think she enjoyed it!

MARK TWAIN

A child's awareness is so
absorbed in his mother that
although he is not consciously
thinking of her, when a problem
arises, the abiding relationship
is that with the mother.

OSWALD CHAMBERS

Grace was all in her steps,
heaven in her eye.
In every gesture,
dignity and love.

JOHN MILTON